FOR ORGANS, PIANOS & ELECTRONIC KEYBOARDS

E-Z PLAY TODAY
31

BIG BAND favorites
2ND EDITION

T0045110

ISBN-13: 978-0-7935-2163-0
ISBN-10: 0-7435-2163-7

HAL•LEONARD®
CORPORATION

7777 W. BLUEMOUND RD. P.O. BOX 13819 MILWAUKEE, WI 53213

For all works contained herein:
Unauthorized copying, arranging, adapting, recording or public performance is an infringement of copyright.
Infringers are liable under the law.

E-Z Play® Today Music Notation © 1975 by HAL LEONARD CORPORATION

E-Z PLAY and EASY ELECTRONIC KEYBOARD MUSIC are registered trademarks of HAL LEONARD CORPORATION.

Visit Hal Leonard Online at
www.halleonard.com

Cherokee
(Indian Love Song)

Registration 2
Rhythm: Swing

Words and Music by
Ray Noble

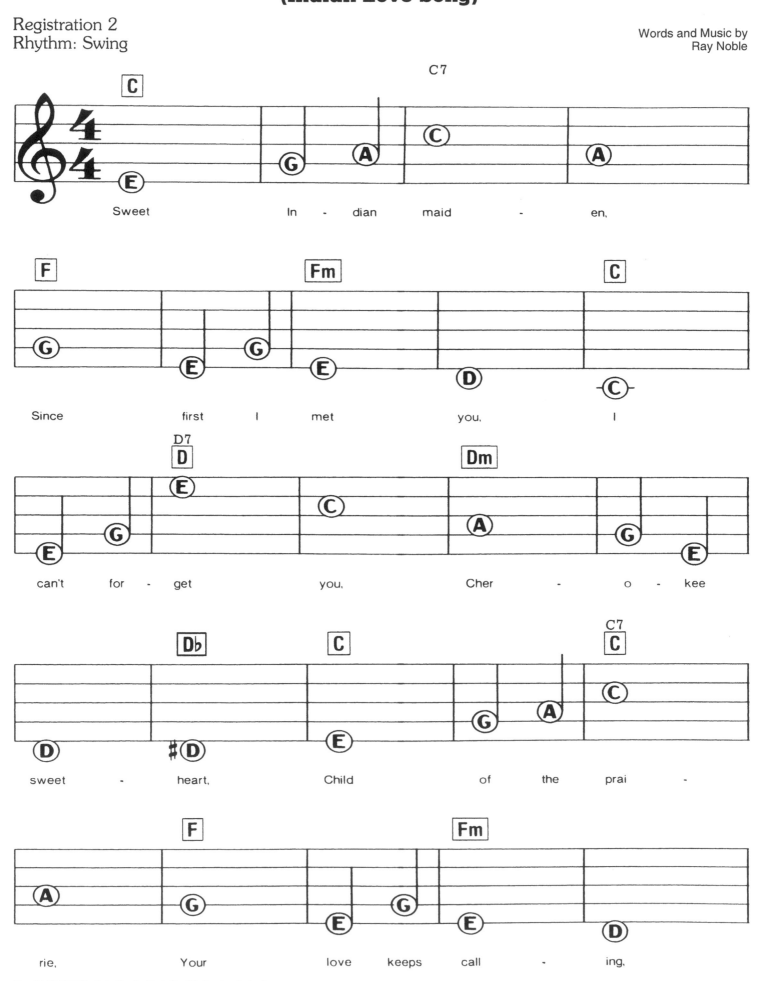

Copyright © 1938 The Peter Maurice Music Co., Ltd., London, England
Copyright Renewed and Assigned to Shapiro, Bernstein & Co., Inc., New York for U.S.A. and Canada
International Copyright Secured   All Rights Reserved
Used by Permission

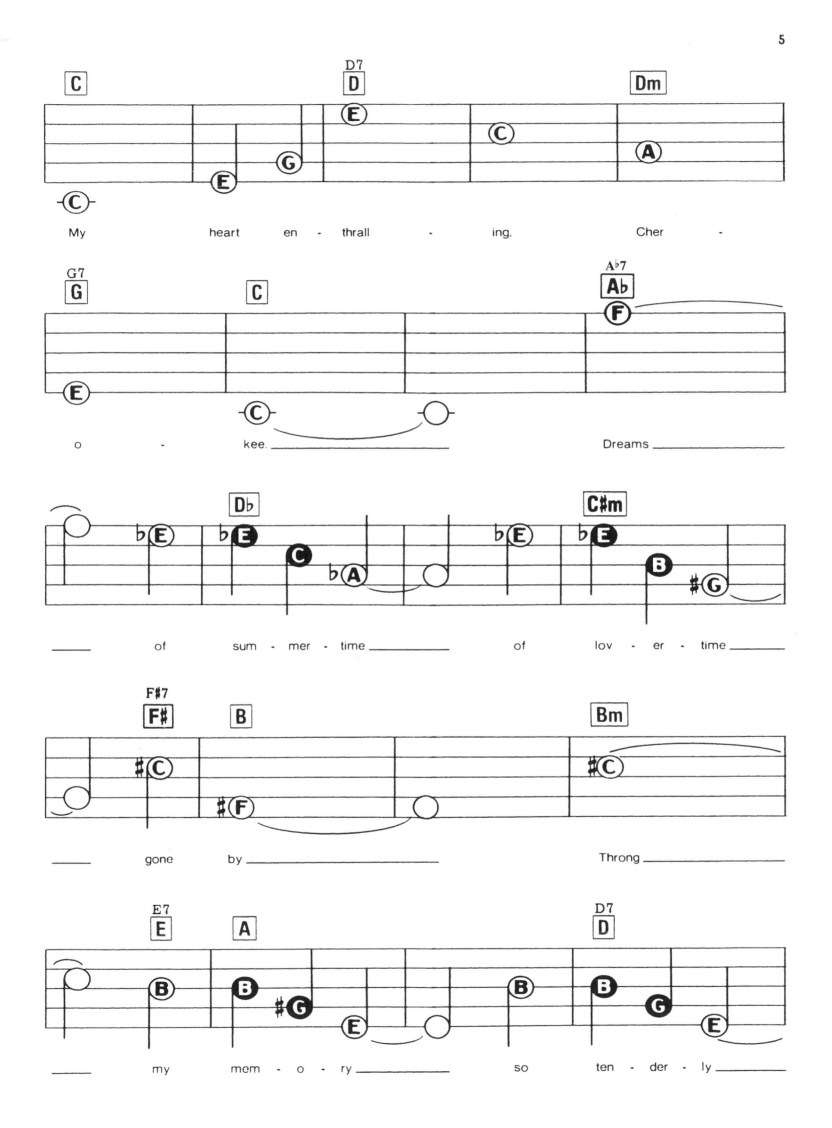

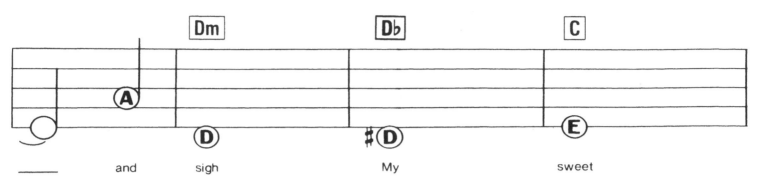

and sigh   My   sweet

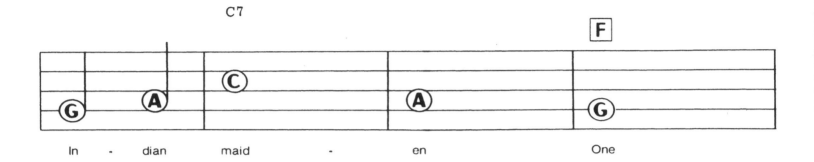

In - dian maid - en   One

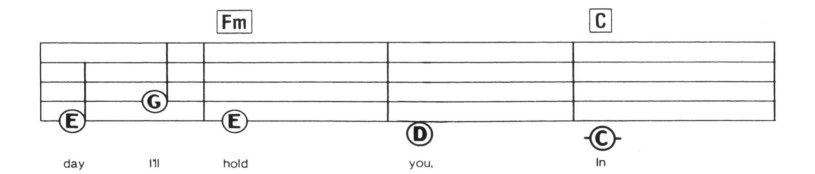

day I'll hold   you,   In

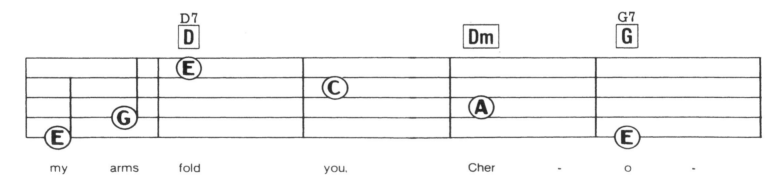

my arms fold   you,   Cher - o -

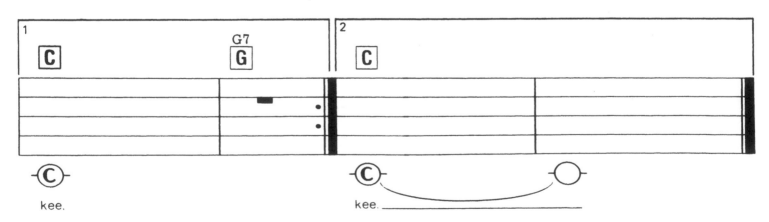

kee.   kee.

My Melancholy Baby

Registration 3
Rhythm: Swing

Words by George Norton
Music by Ernie Burnett

Copyright © 1994 by HAL LEONARD CORPORATION
International Copyright Secured   All Rights Reserved

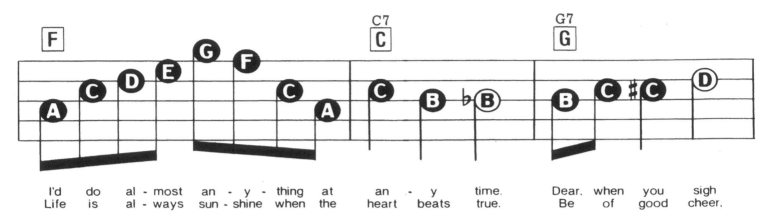

I'd do al - most an - y - thing at an - y time. Dear, when you sigh
Life is al - ways sun - shine when the heart beats true. Be of good cheer,

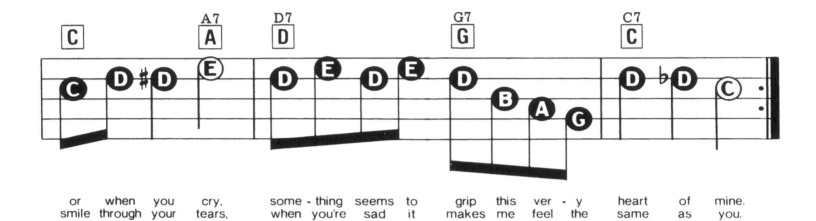

or when you cry, some - thing seems to grip this ver - y heart of mine.
smile through your tears, when you're sad it makes me feel the same as you.

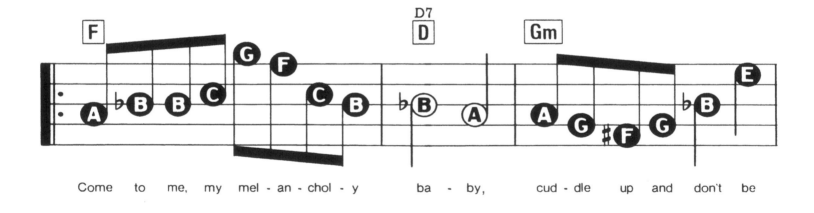

Come to me, my mel - an - chol - y ba - by, cud - dle up and don't be

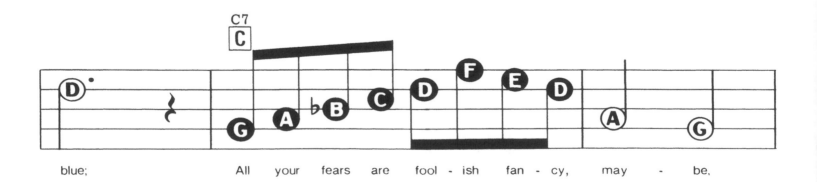

blue; All your fears are fool - ish fan - cy, may - be,

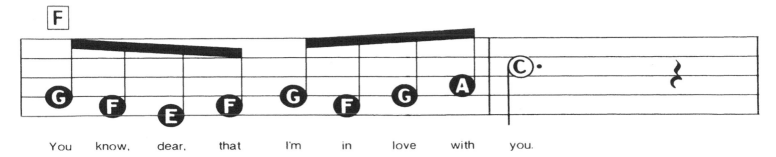

You know, dear, that I'm in love with you.

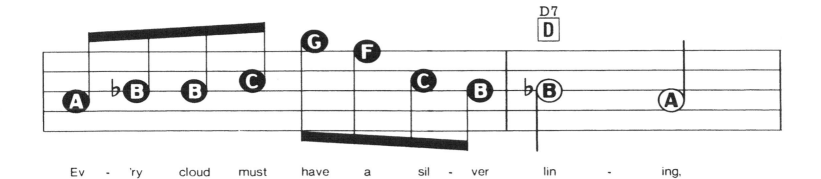

Ev - 'ry cloud must have a sil - ver lin - ing,

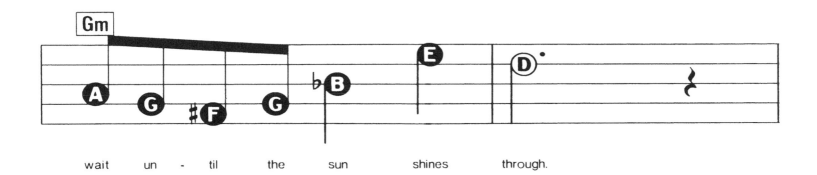

wait un - til the sun shines through.

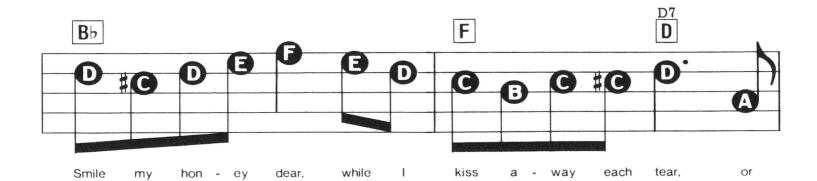

Smile my hon - ey dear, while I kiss a - way each tear, or

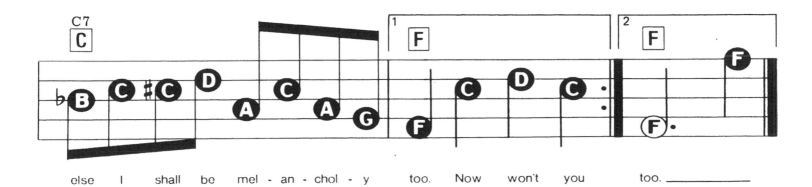

else I shall be mel - an - chol - y too. Now won't you too. _____

I'll Be Around

Registration 10
Rhythm: Ballad

Words and Music by
Alec Wilder

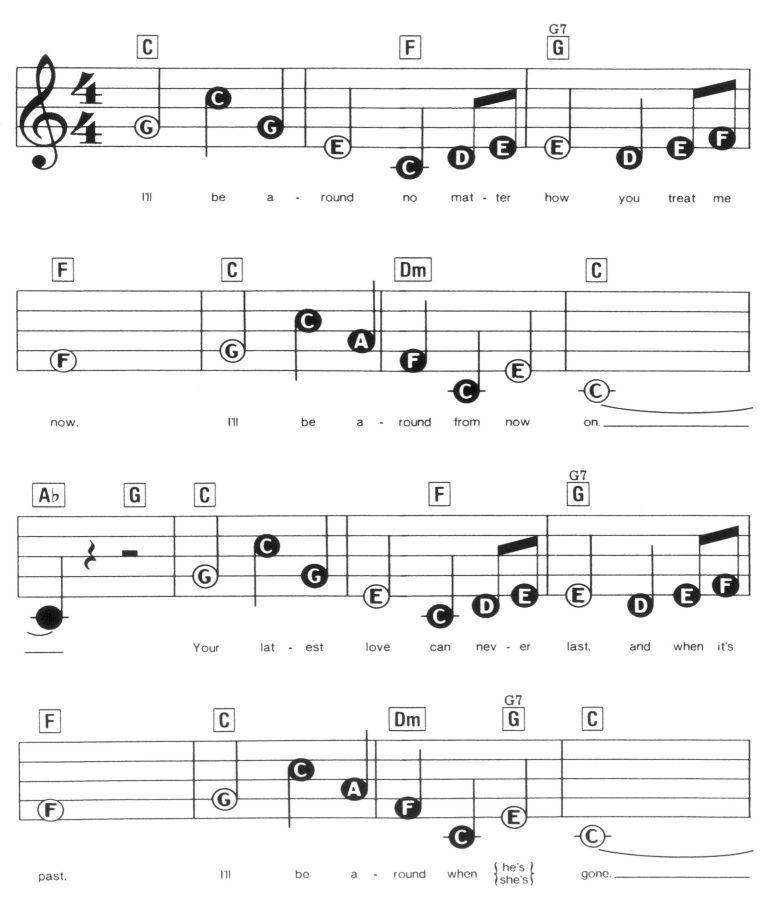

TRO - © Copyright 1942 (Renewed) Ludlow Music, Inc., New York, NY
International Copyright Secured
All Rights Reserved Including Public Performance For Profit
Used by Permission

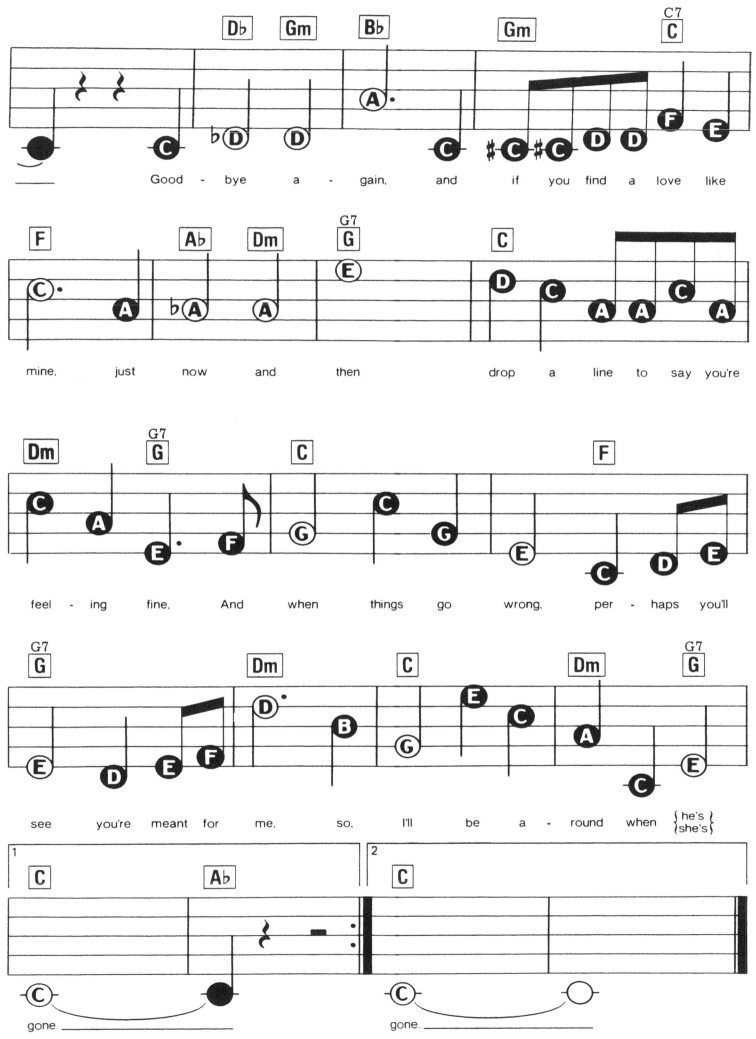

I'll Never Smile Again

Registration 4
Rhythm: Fox Trot or Swing

Words and Music by
Ruth Lowe

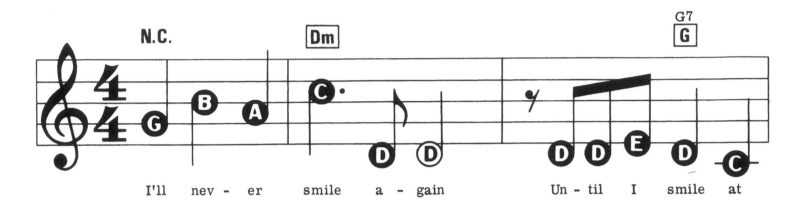

I'll nev - er smile a - gain Un - til I smile at

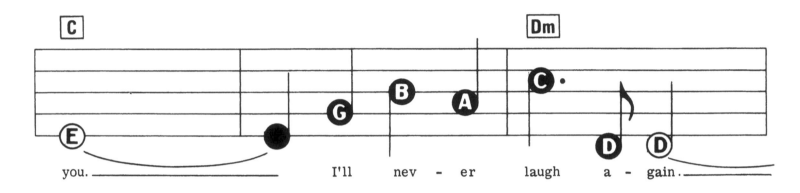

you. _____ I'll nev - er laugh a - gain. _____

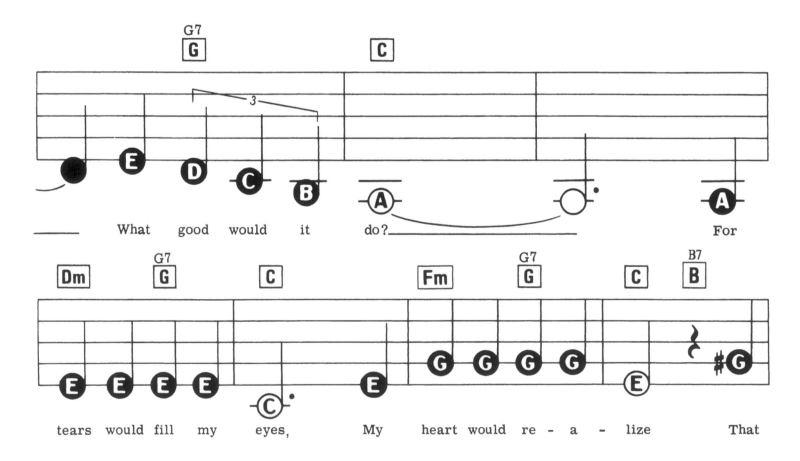

_____ What good would it do? _____ For

tears would fill my eyes, My heart would re - a - lize That

Copyright © 1939 UNIVERSAL MUSIC CORP.
Copyright Renewed
All Rights Reserved   Used by Permission

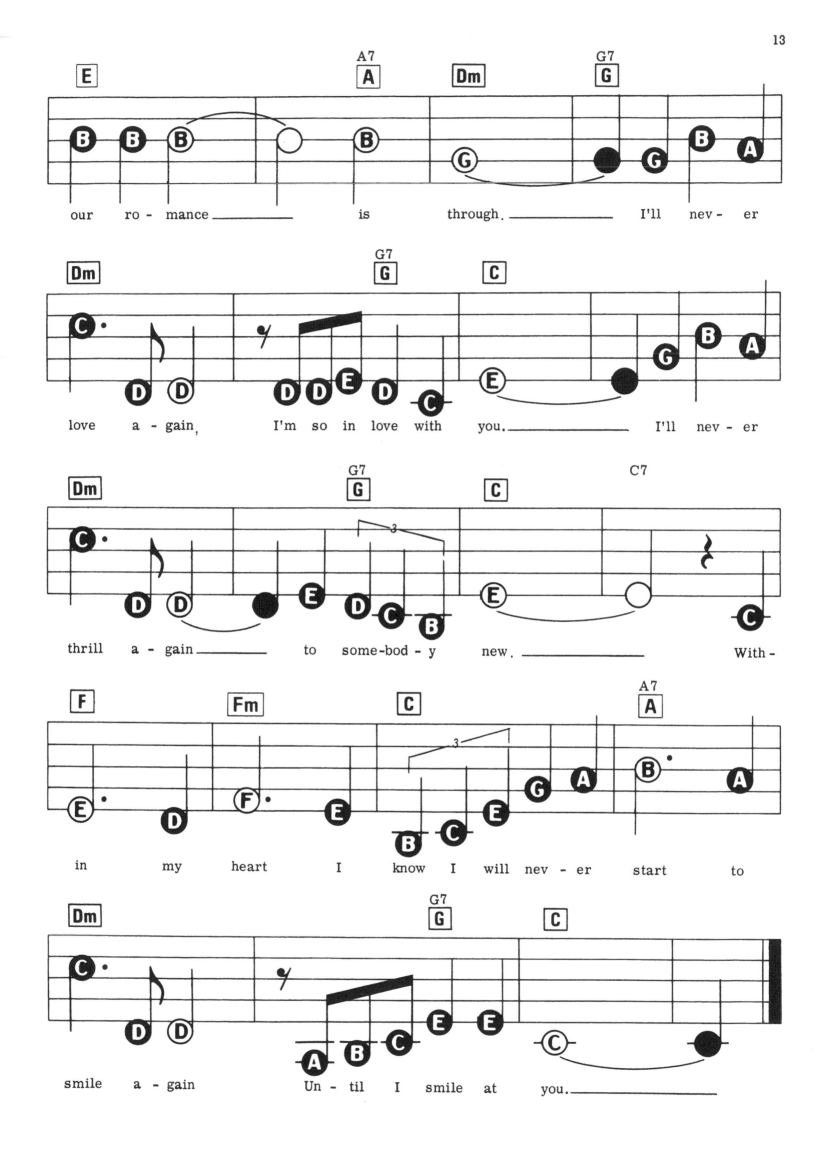

I'll Remember April

Registration 3
Rhythm: Swing

Words and Music by Pat Johnson,
Don Raye and Gene De Paul

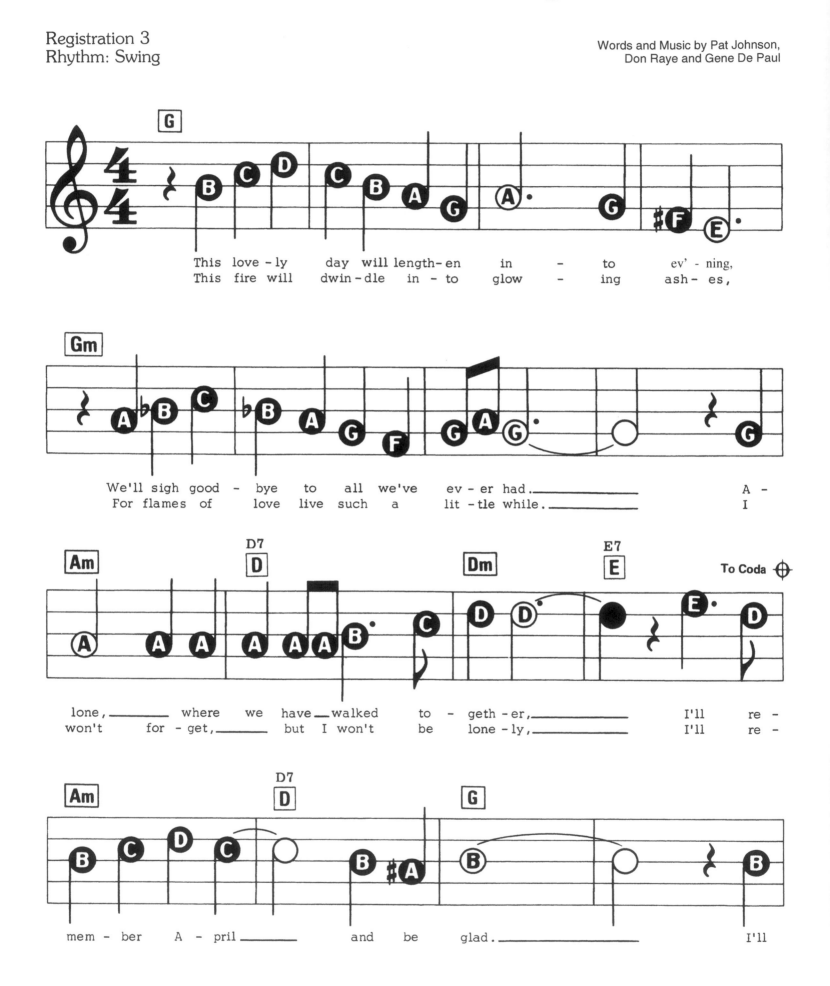

© 1941, 1942 (Renewed) PIC CORPORATION and UNIVERSAL MUSIC CORP.
All Rights Reserved

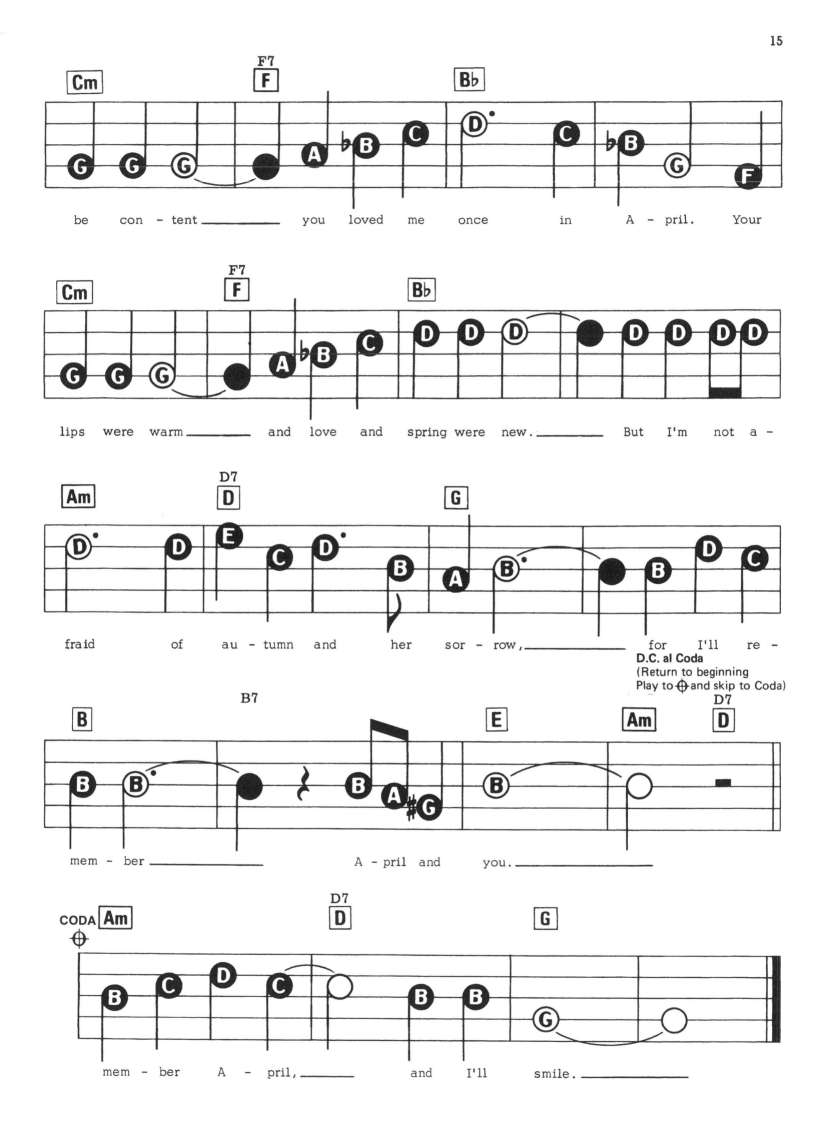

In a Little Spanish Town
('Twas on a Night Like This)

Registration 3
Rhythm: Waltz

Words by Sam M. Lewis and Joe Young
Music by Mabel Wayne

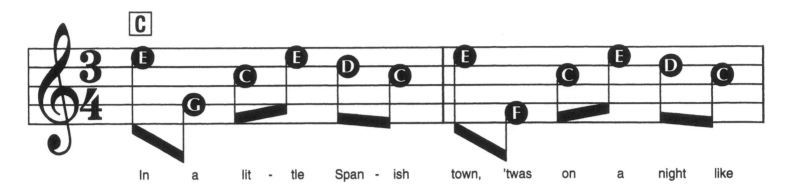

In a lit - tle Span - ish town, 'twas on a night like

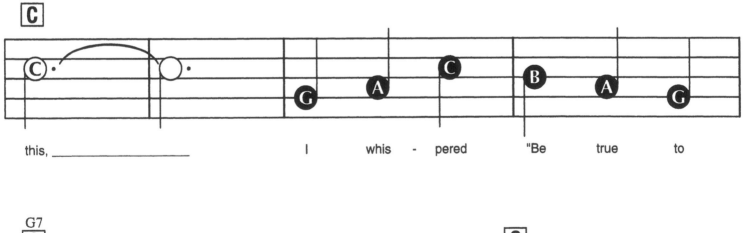

this, _____ stars were peek - a - boo - ing down, 'twas on a night like

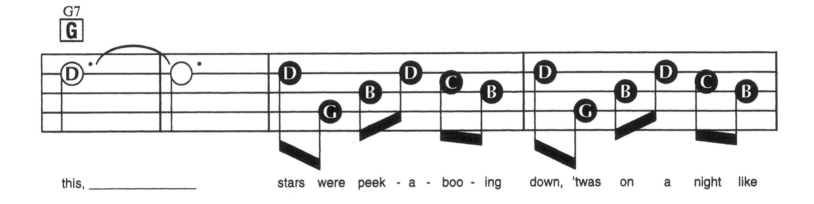

this, _____ I whis - pered "Be true to

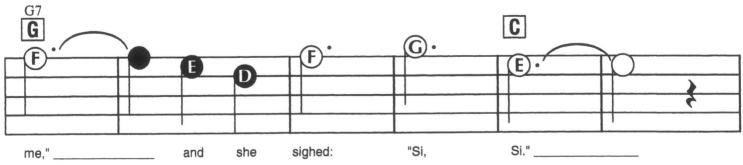

me," _____ and she sighed: "Si, Si." _____

© 1926 LEO FEIST, INC.
© Renewed 1954 WAROCK CORP. and LEO FEIST, INC.
All Rights Reserved

17

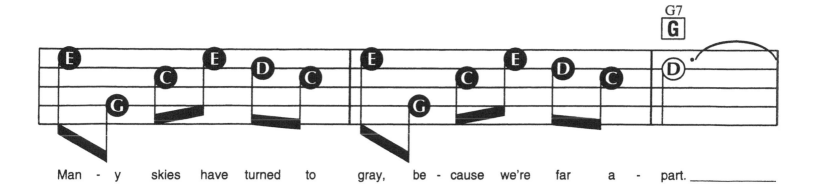

Man - y skies have turned to gray, be - cause we're far a - part. _____

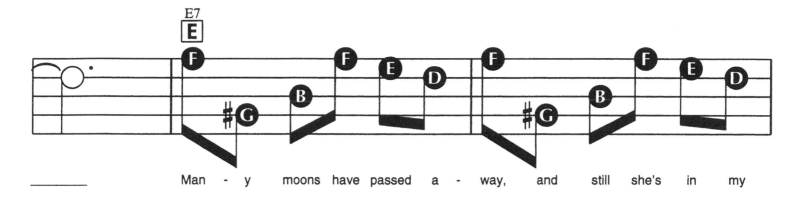

_____ Man - y moons have passed a - way, and still she's in my

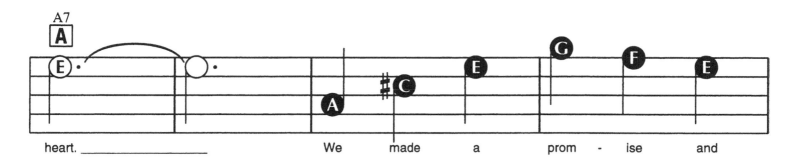

heart. _____ We made a prom - ise and

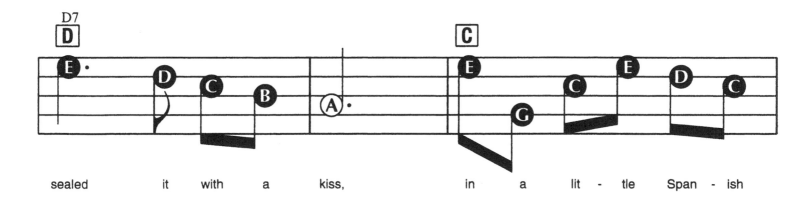

sealed it with a kiss, in a lit - tle Span - ish

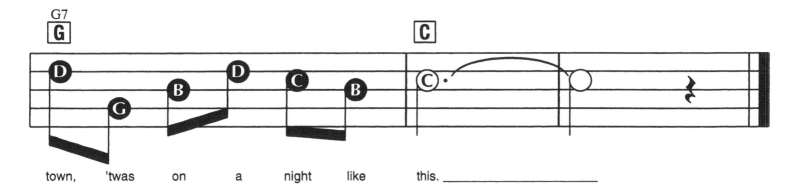

town, 'twas on a night like this. _____

It's the Talk of the Town

Registration 4
Rhythm: Fox Trot or Swing

Words by Marty Symes and Al Neiburg
Music by Jerry Livingston

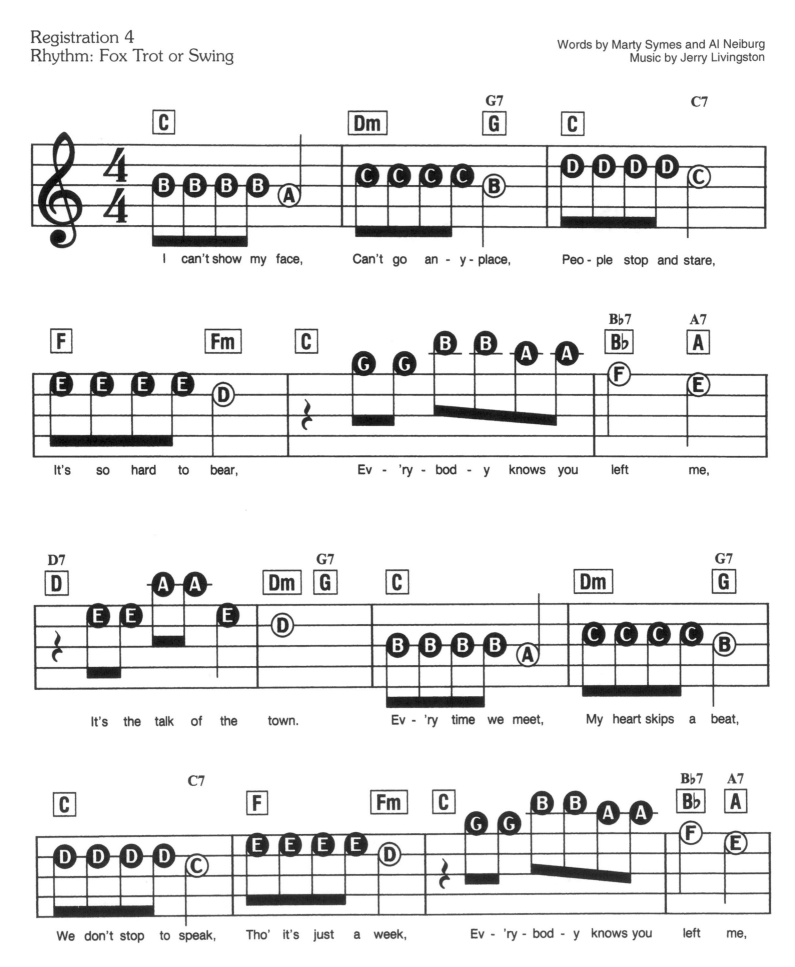

Copyright © 1933 (Renewed) by Music Sales Corporation (ASCAP) and Hallmark Music Publishing Company (ASCAP)
All Rights for Hallmark Music Publishing Company Controlled and Administered by Spirit Two Music, Inc. (ASCAP)
International Copyright Secured   All Rights Reserved
Reprinted by Permission

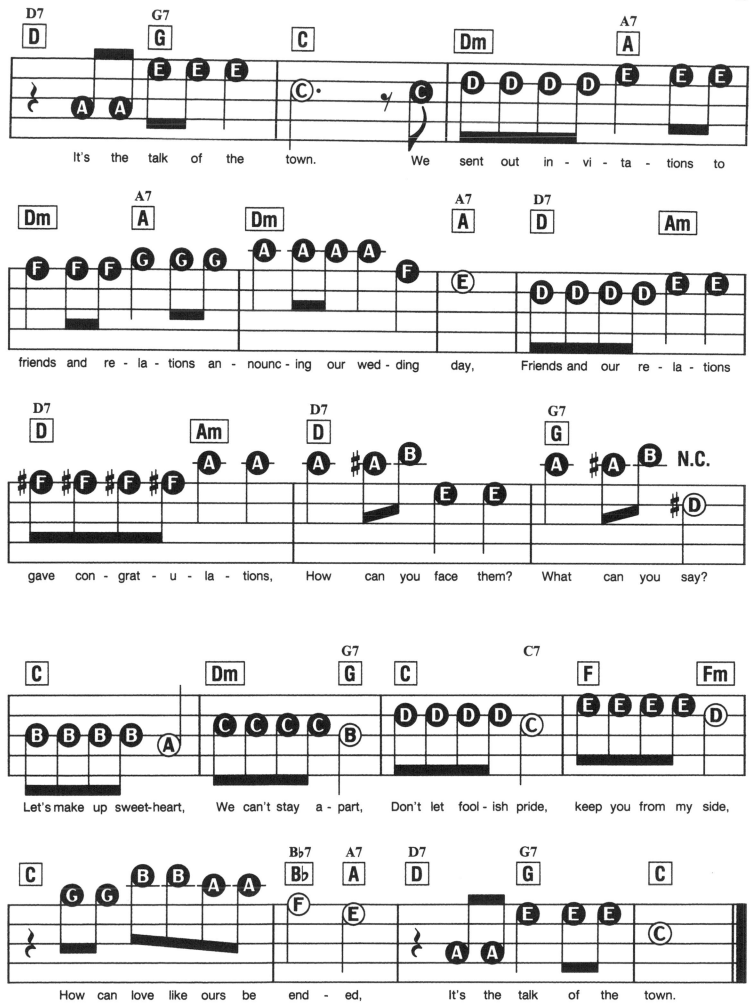

Little White Lies

Registration 2
Rhythm: Fox Trot or Swing

Words and Music by
Walter Donaldson

Copyright © 1930 (Renewed) by Donaldson Publishing Co. and Dreyer Music Co.
All Rights for Dreyer Music Co. Administered by Larry Spier, Inc., New York
International Copyright Secured All Rights Reserved

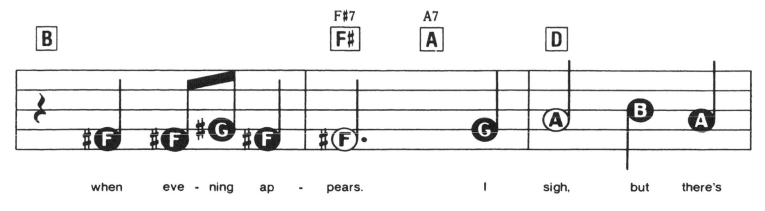

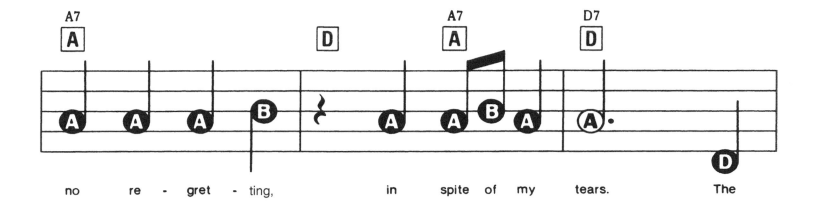

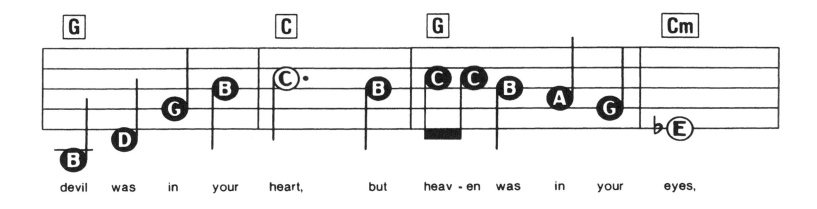

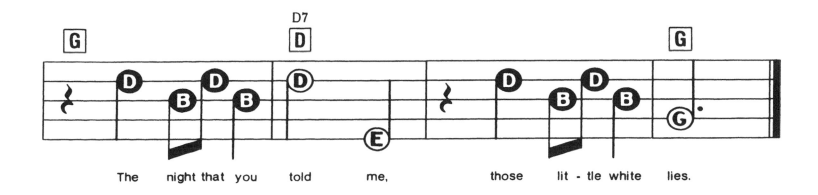

21

Manhattan
from the Broadway Musical THE GARRICK GAIETIES

Registration 7
Rhythm: Fox Trot

Words by Lorenz Hart
Music by Richard Rodgers

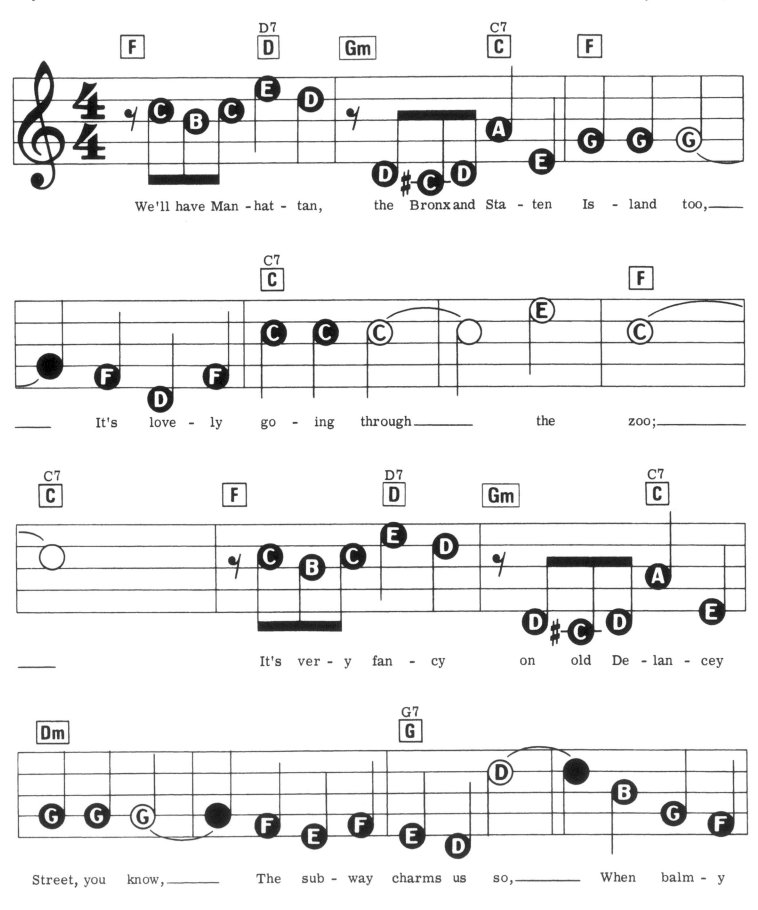

Copyright © 1925 by Edward B. Marks Music Company
Copyright Renewed
International Copyright Secured   All Rights Reserved
Used by Permission

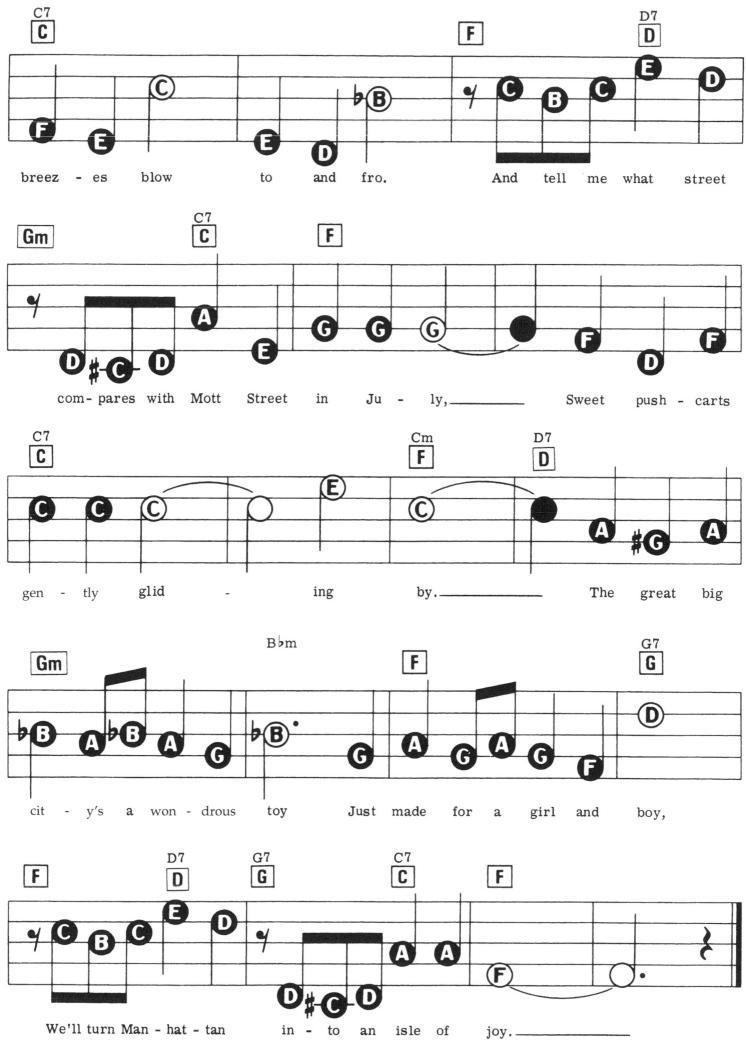

On the Sunny Side of the Street

Registration 7
Rhythm: Fox Trot or Swing

Lyric by Dorothy Fields
Music by Jimmy McHugh

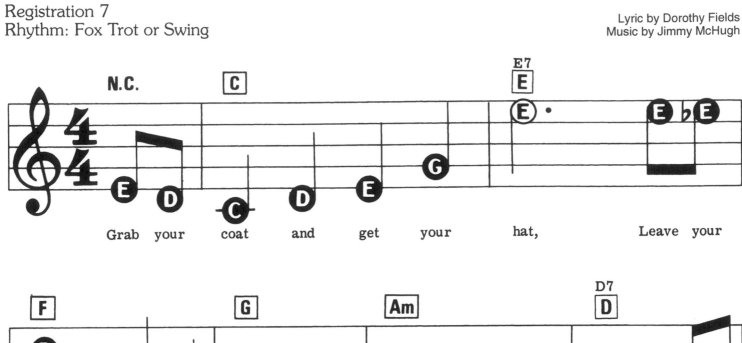

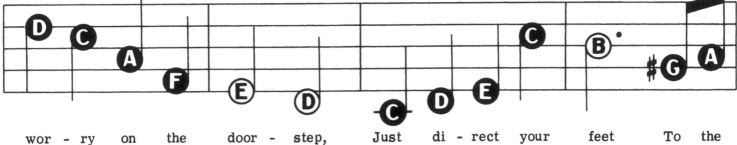

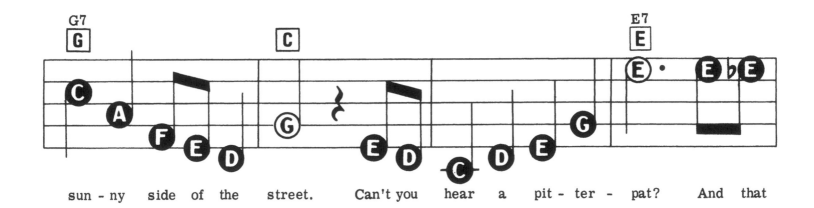

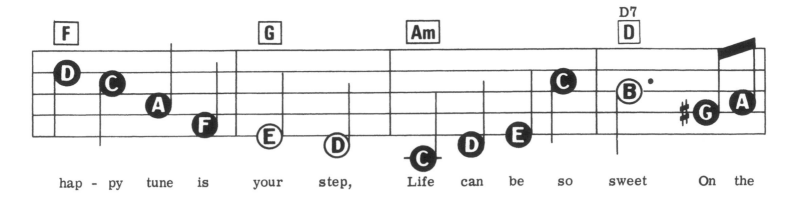

Copyright © 1930 Shapiro, Bernstein & Co., Inc., New York and Cotton Club Publishing for the USA
Copyright Renewed
All Rights for Cotton Club Publishing Controlled and Administered by EMI April Music Inc.
International Copyright Secured   All Rights Reserved
Used by Permission

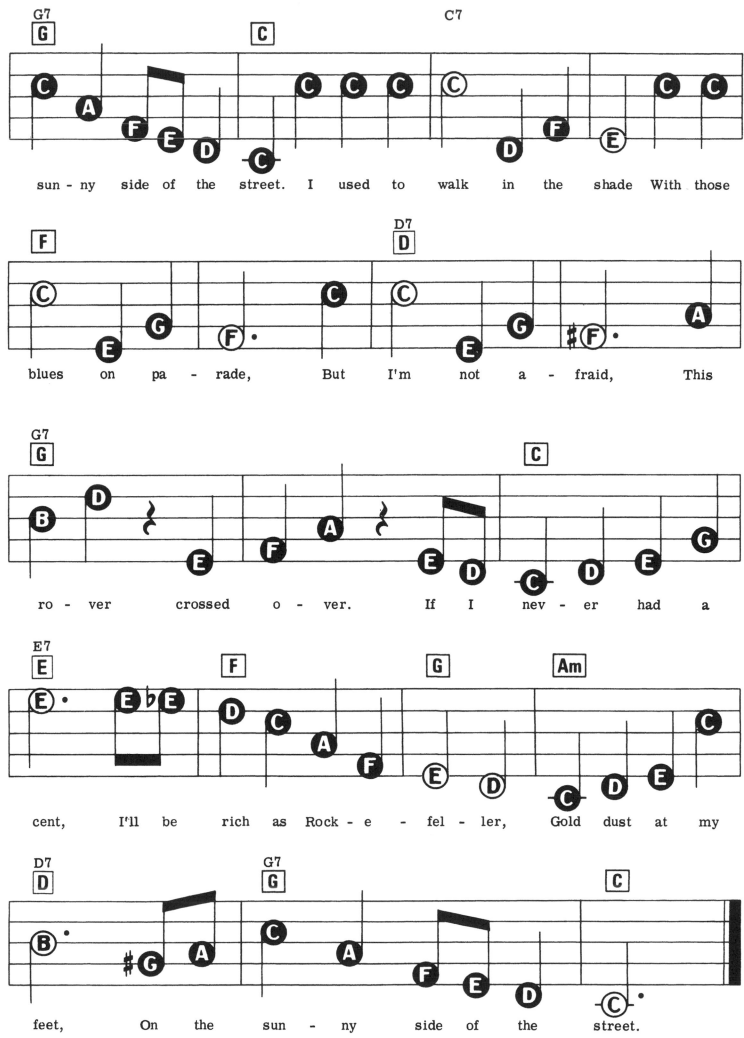

Penthouse Serenade

Registration 1
Rhythm: Swing

Words and Music by Will Jason
and Val Burton

Just pic - ture a pent - house way up in the sky, with
all of so - ci - e - ty we'll stay a - loof with and

hing - es on chim - neys for stars to go by. A
live in pro - pri - e - ty there on the roof. Two

sweet slice of heav - en for just you and I when we're a -
heav - en - ly her - mits we will be in truth when when

lone. From we're a - lone. We'll see life's mad

Copyright © 1931 by Famous Music Corporation
Copyright Renewed; extended term of Copyright deriving from Val Burton and Will Jason
  assigned and effective July 13, 1987 to Range Road Music Inc. and Quartet Music
All Rights Administered in the U.S. by Range Road Music Inc.
International Copyright Secured   All Rights Reserved
Used by Permission

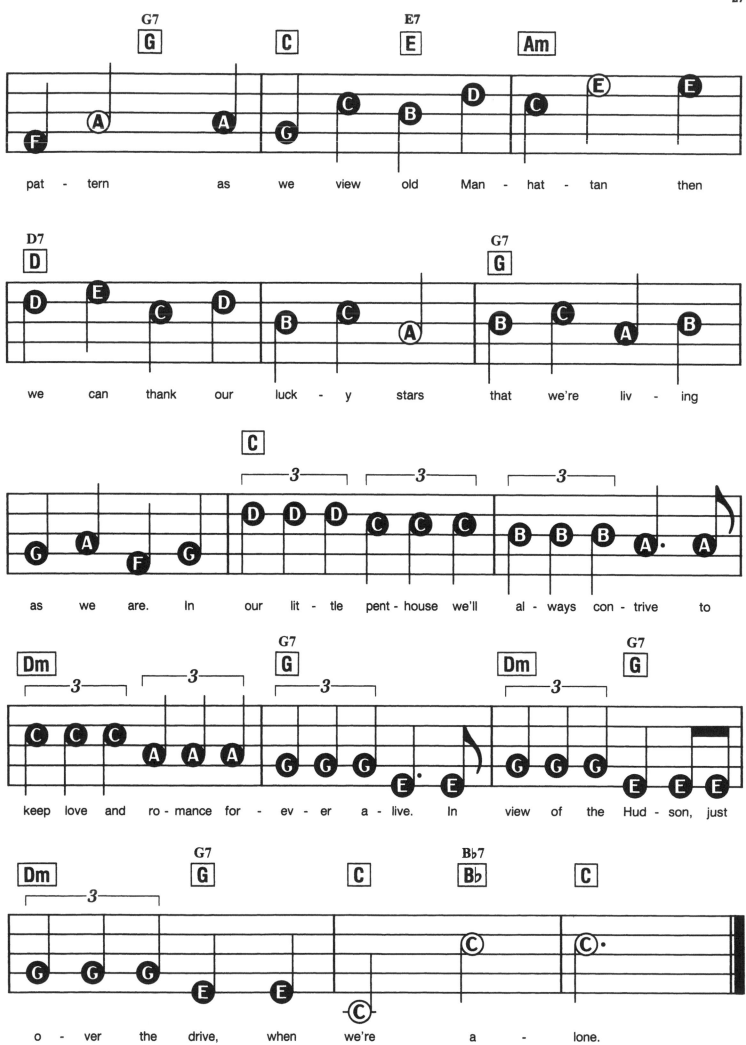

Put Your Arms Around Me, Honey

Registration 9
Rhythm: Fox Trot

Words by Junie McCree
Music by Albert von Tilzer

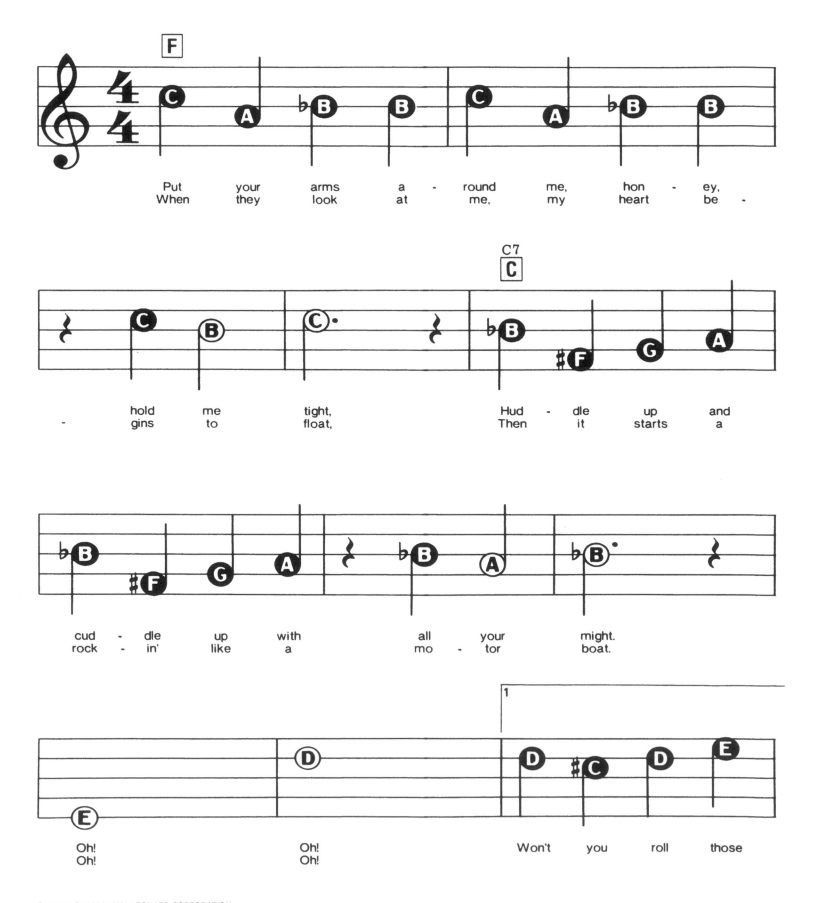

Copyright © 1996 by HAL LEONARD CORPORATION
International Copyright Secured   All Rights Reserved

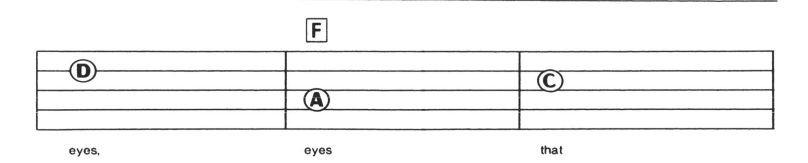

eyes,   eyes   that

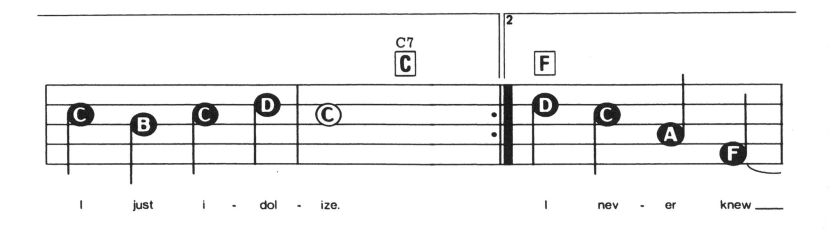

I just i - dol - ize.   I nev - er knew ___

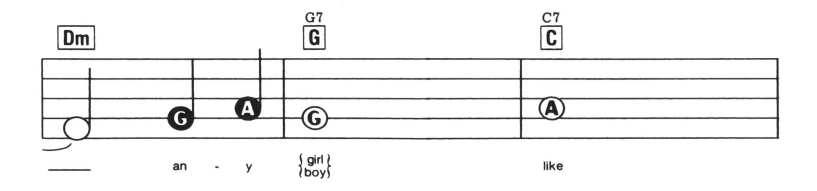

___   an - y {girl}{boy}   like

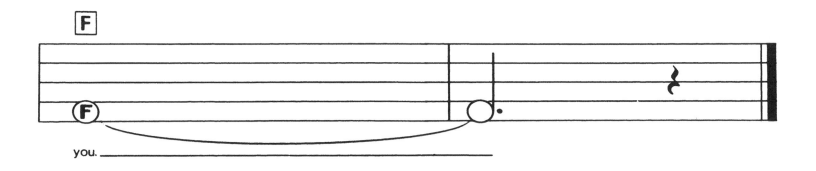

you. _____

Somebody Loves You

Registration 8
Rhythm: Fox Trot or Swing

Words by Charlie Tobias
Music by Peter De Rose

Some - bod - y loves you, I want you to

know. Longs to be near you wher -

ev - er you go, Some - bod - y loves you and

right from the start, Hap - pi - ness flew in - to

some - one's heart;_____ Some - bod - y loves you each

© 1932 (Renewed) EDWIN H. MORRIS & COMPANY, A Division of MPL Music Publishing, Inc.
All Rights Reserved

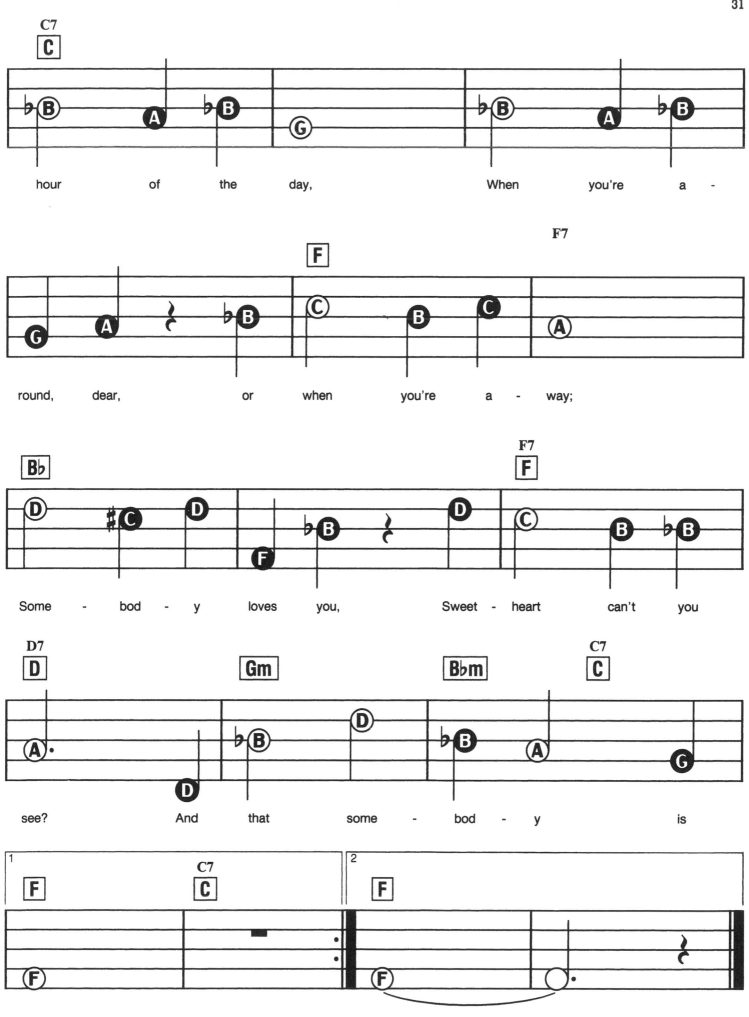

Stompin' at the Savoy

Registration 2
Rhythm: Swing

Words by Andy Razaf
Music by Benny Goodman,
Edgar Sampson and Chick Webb

Sa - voy, the home of sweet ro - mance; Sa -
voy, it wins you at a glance; Sa - voy, gives hap - py feet a
chance to dance. Your form just like a cling - in'
vine, Your lips so warm and sweet as wine, Your
cheek so soft and close to mine, di - vine!

Copyright © 1936 by EMI Robbins Catalog Inc.
Copyright Renewed by Rytvoc, Inc., Ragbag Music Publishing Corporation (ASCAP), EMI Robbins Music Corporation and Razaf Music Co.
International Copyright Secured   All Rights Reserved
Used by Permission

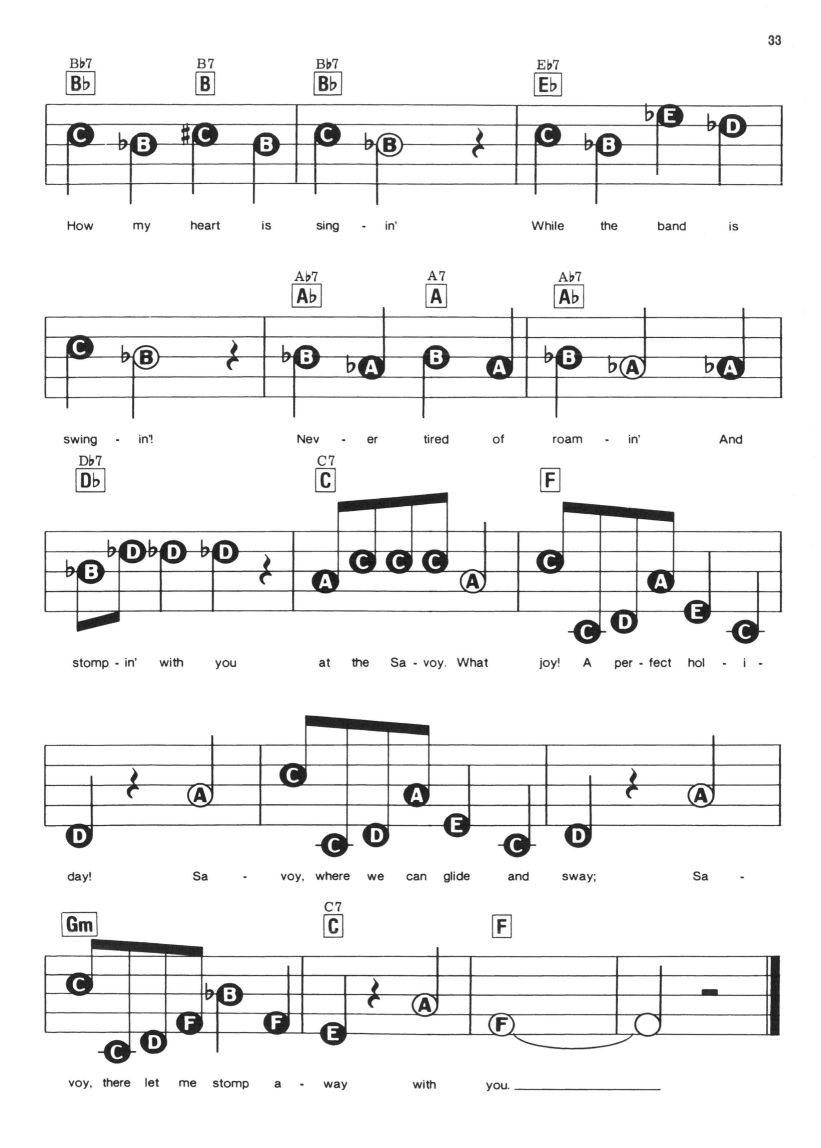

A String of Pearls
from THE GLENN MILLER STORY

Registration 4
Rhythm: Swing

Words by Eddie De Lange
Music by Jerry Gray

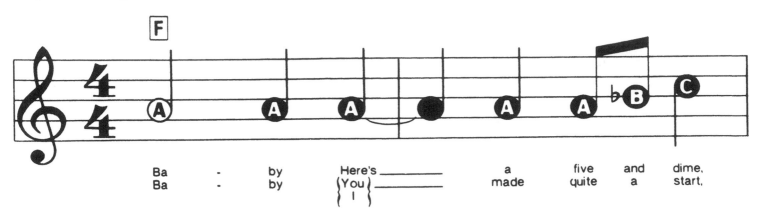

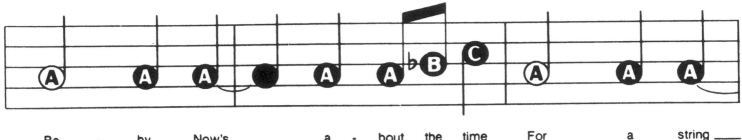

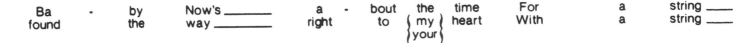

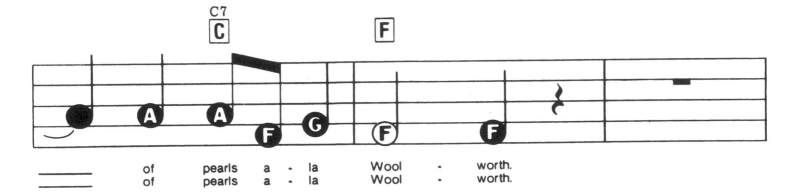

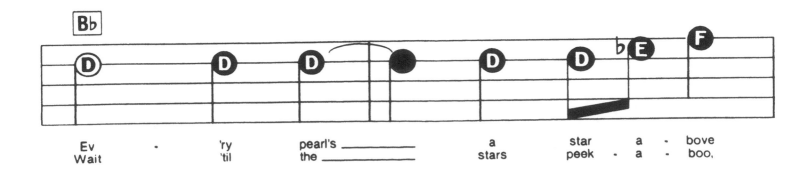

Copyright © 1941, 1942 by Mutual Music Society, Inc.
Copyright Renewed, Assigned to Chappell & Co. and Scarsdale Music Corp.
International Copyright Secured   All Rights Reserved
Used by Permission

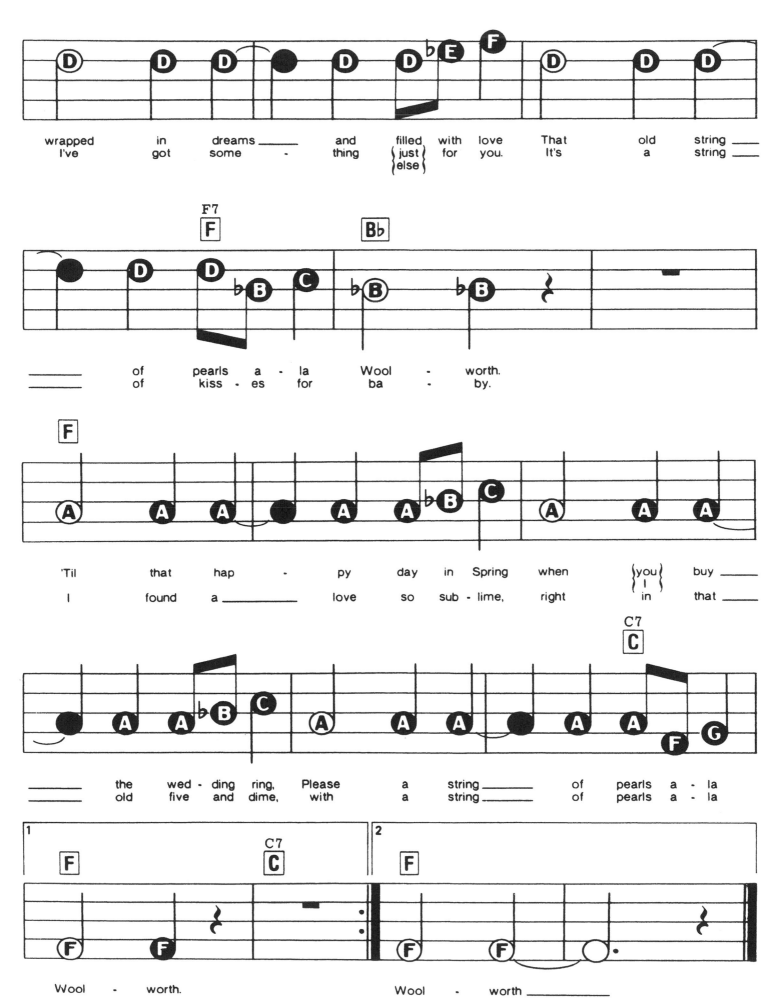

Sunrise Serenade

Registration 8
Rhythm: Swing or Fox Trot

Lyric by Jack Lawrence
Music by Frankie Carle

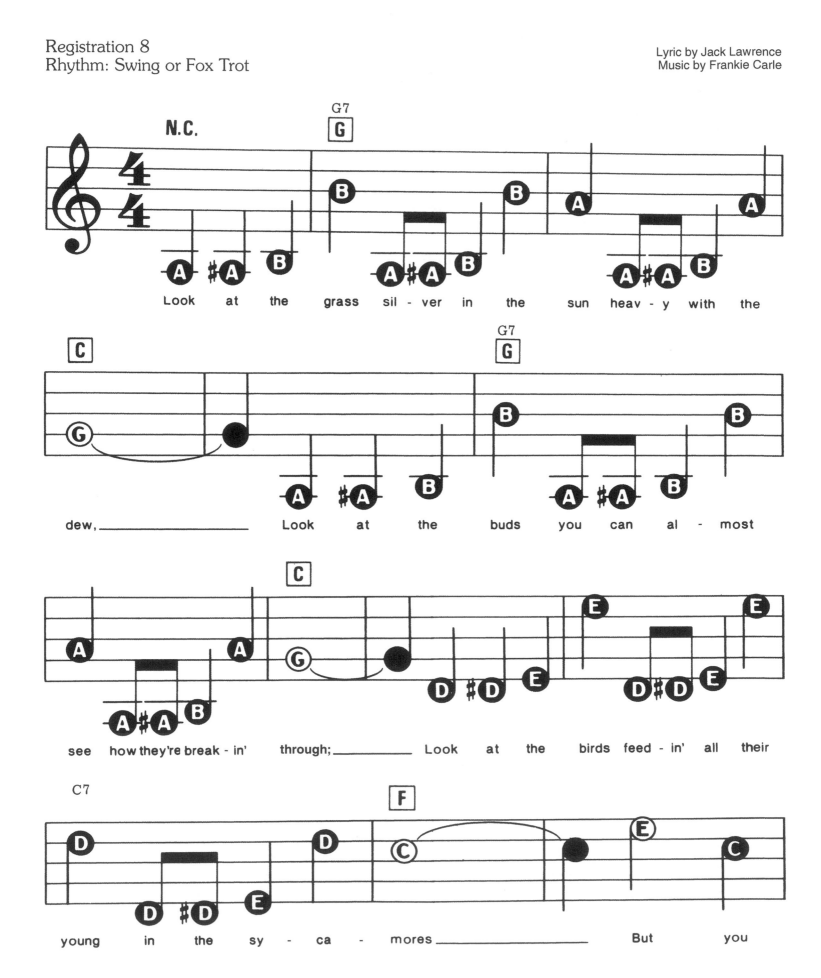

Copyright © 1938, 1939 Jewel Music Publishing Co., Inc.
Copyright renewed; extended term of Copyright deriving from Jack Lawrence assigned and effective April 20, 1995 to Range Road Music Inc.
Extended term of Copyright deriving from Frankie Carle assigned to Music Sales Corporation (ASCAP)
International Copyright Secured All Rights Reserved
Used by Permission

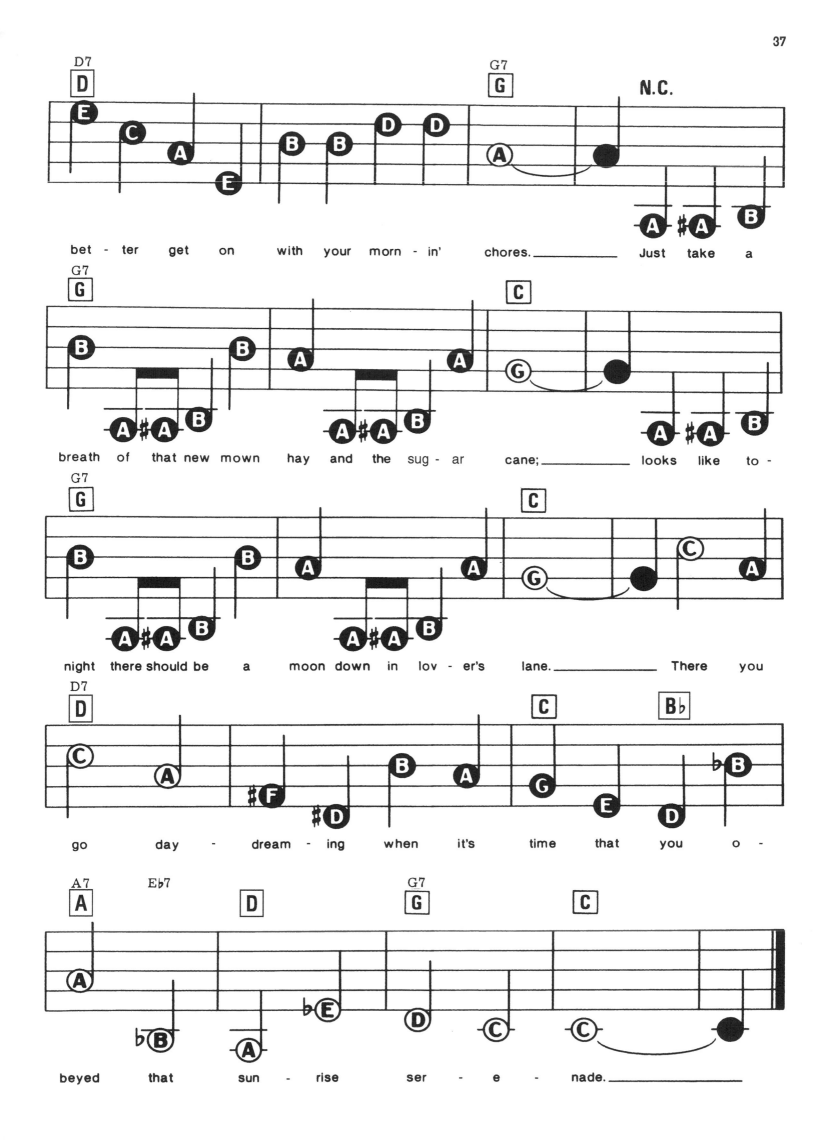

There'll Be Some Changes Made

from ALL THAT JAZZ

Registration 7
Rhythm: Swing or Jazz

Words by Billy Higgins
Music by W. Benton Overstreet

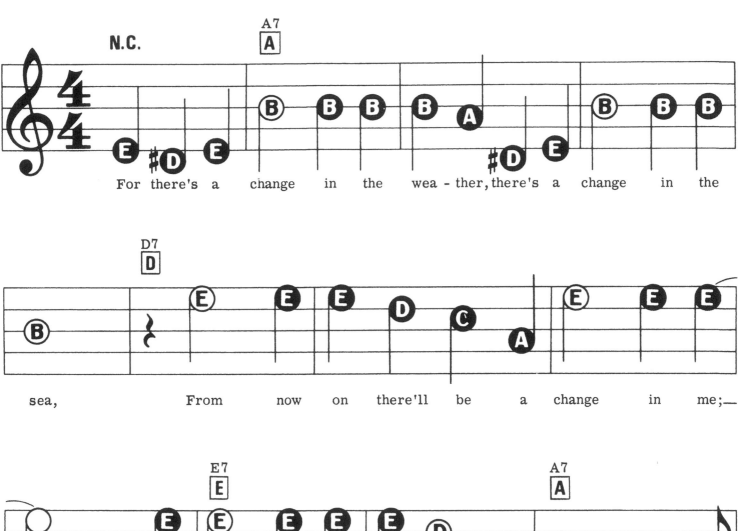

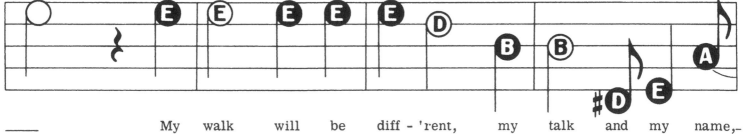

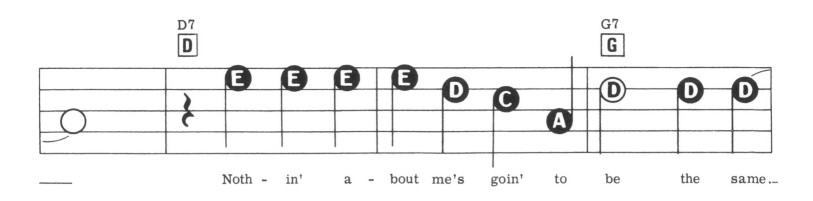

Copyright © 2007 by HAL LEONARD CORPORATION
International Copyright Secured   All Rights Reserved

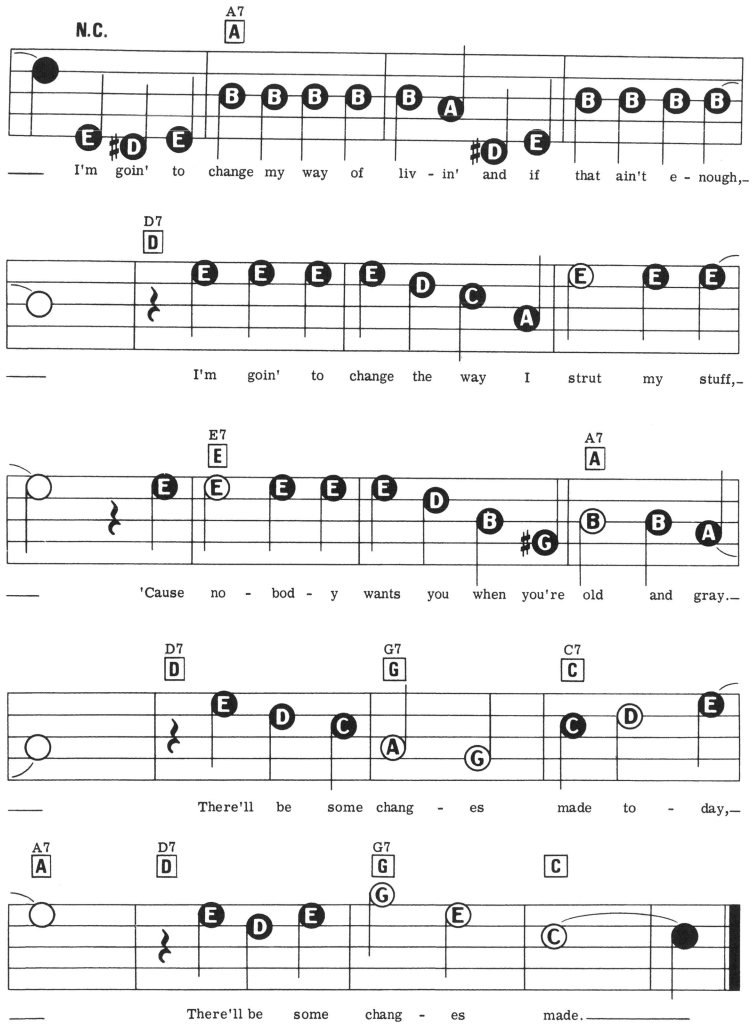

Tuxedo Junction

Registration 1
Rhythm: Fox Trot or Swing

Words by Buddy Feyne
Music by Erskine Hawkins,
William Johnson and Julian Dash

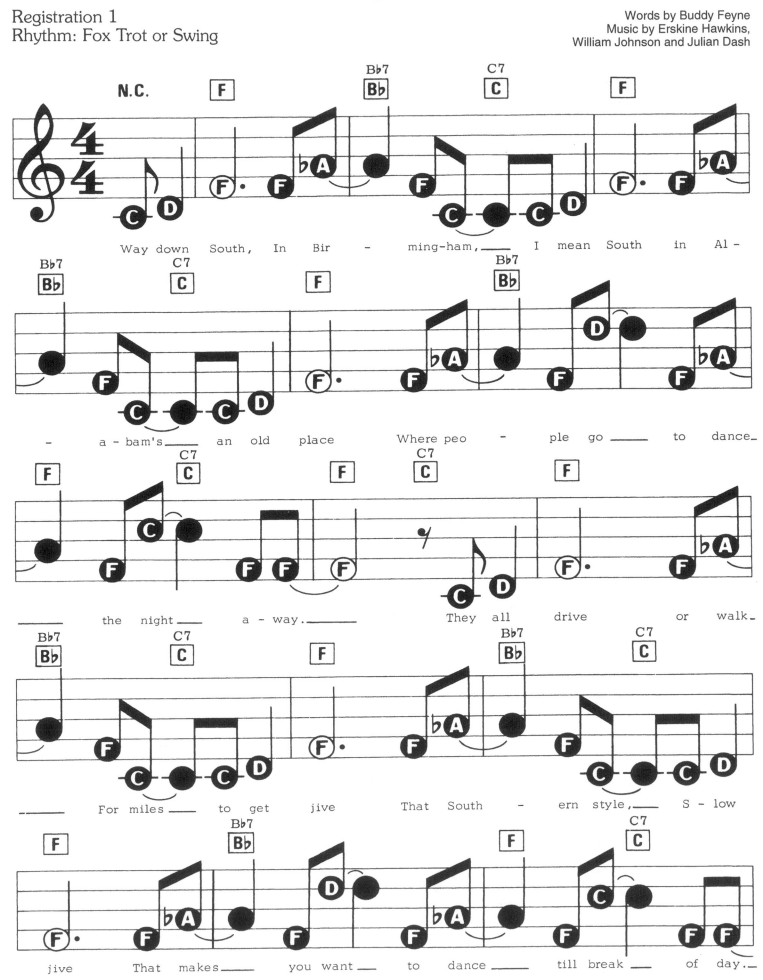

Copyright © 1939, 1940 (Renewed) by Music Sales Corporation (ASCAP) and Rytvoc, Inc.
International Copyright Secured All Rights Reserved
Reprinted by Permission

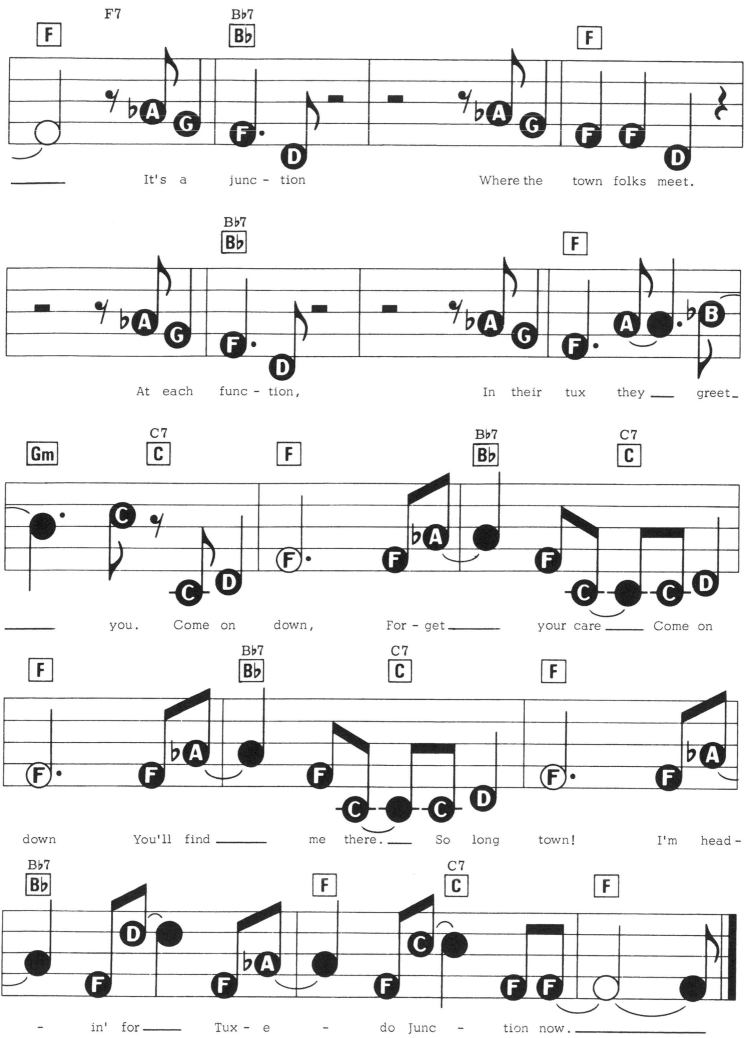

Yes Indeed

Registration 7
Rhythm: March

Words and Music by
Sy Oliver

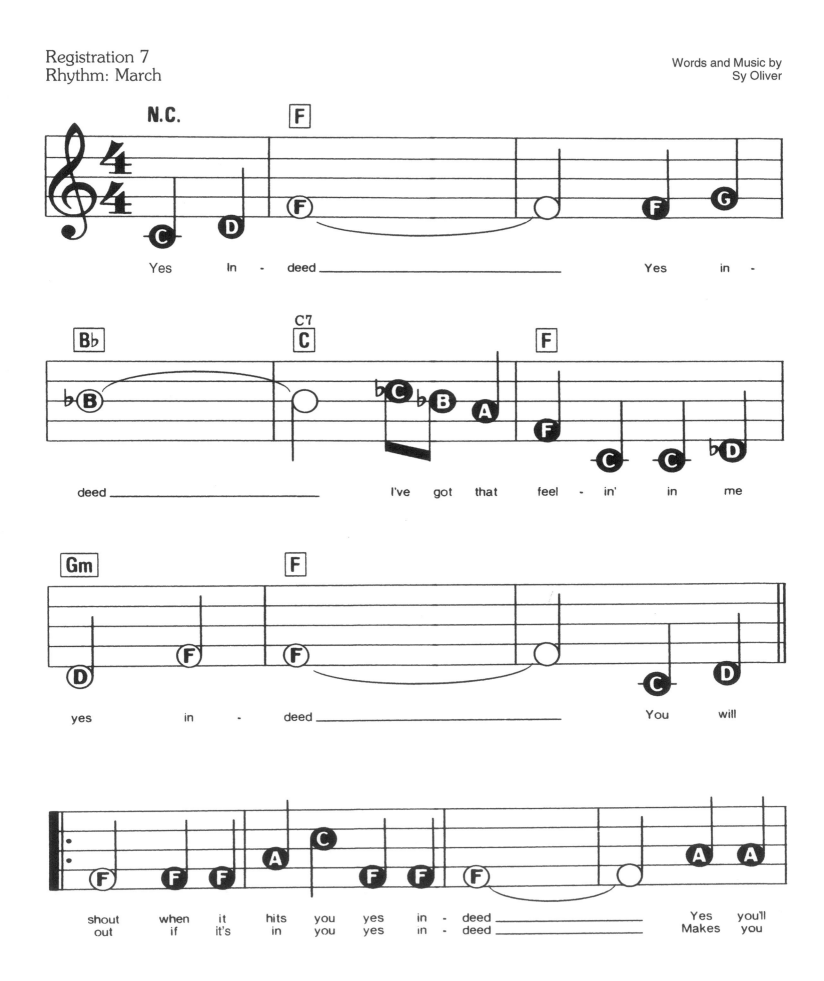

Copyright © 1940 (Renewed) by Embassy Music Corporation (BMI)
International Copyright Secured   All Rights Reserved
Reprinted by Permission

You're Driving Me Crazy!

(What Did I Do?)

Registration 8
Rhythm: Ballad or Fox Trot

Words and Music by
Walter Donaldson

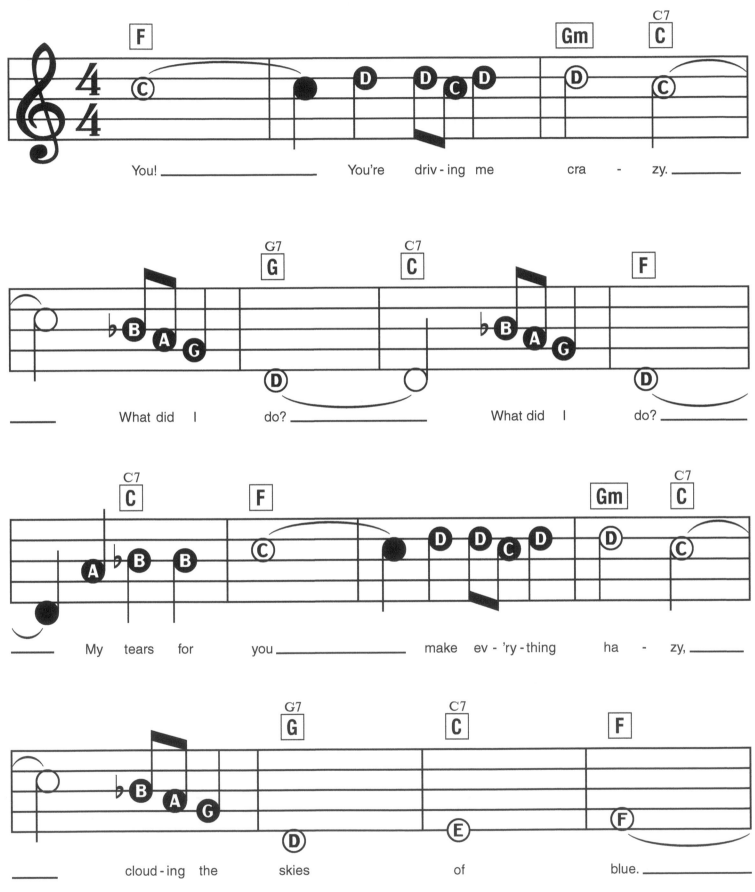

Copyright © 1930 (Renewed) by Donaldson Publishing Co. and Dreyer Music Co.
All Rights for Dreyer Music Co. Administered by Larry Spier, Inc., New York
International Copyright Secured All Rights Reserved

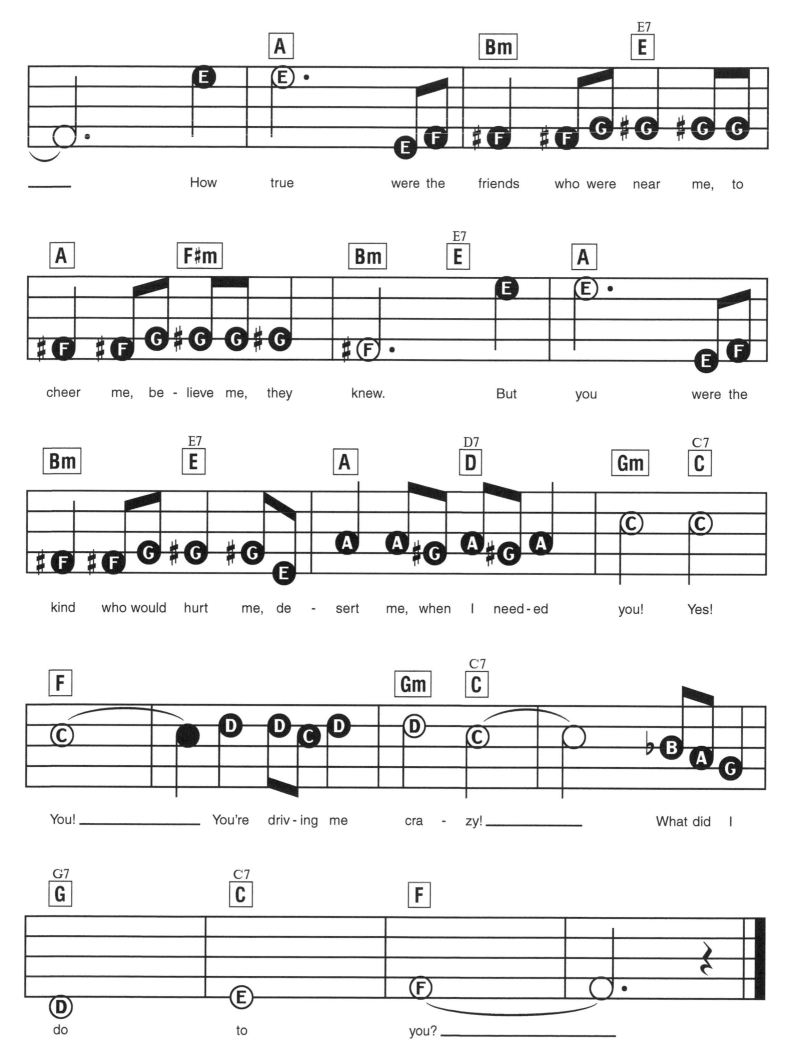

Twelfth Street Rag

Registration 5
Rhythm: Shuffle or Swing

By Euday L. Bowman

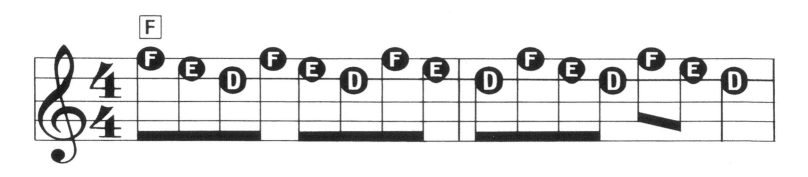

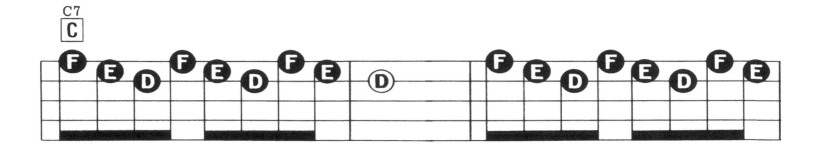

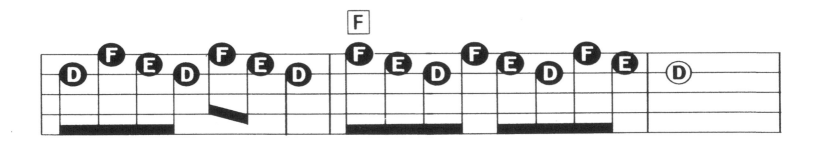

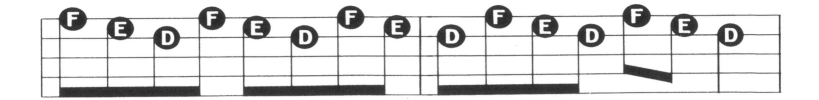

Copyright © 1994 by HAL LEONARD CORPORATION
International Copyright Secured   All Rights Reserved

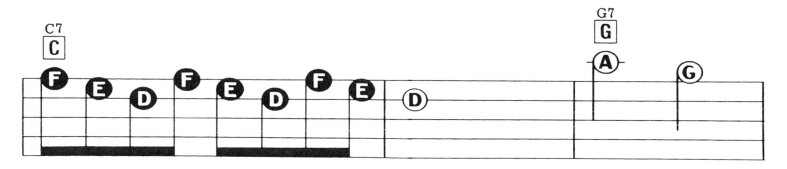

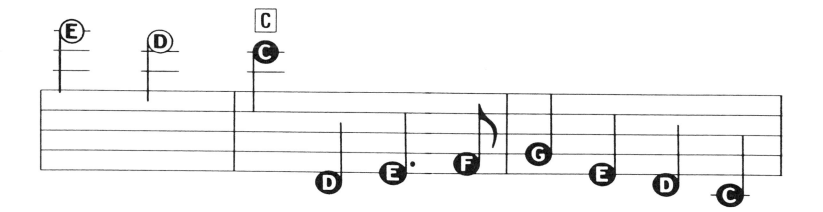

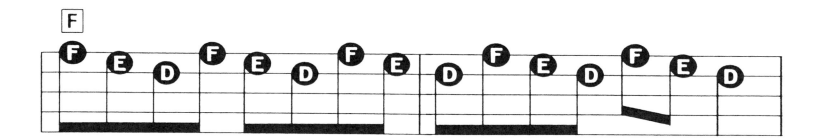

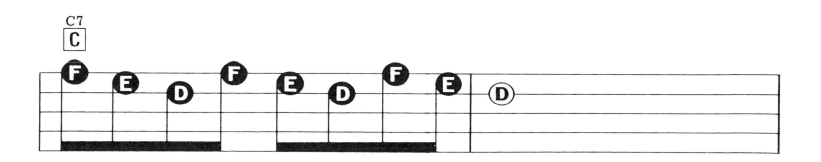

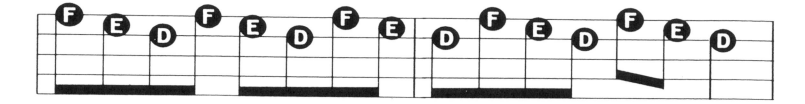

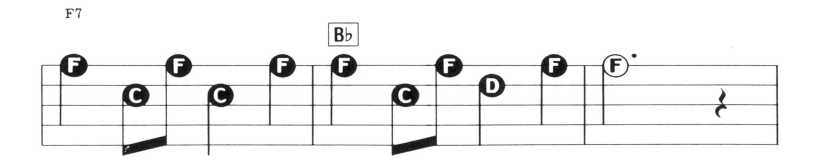

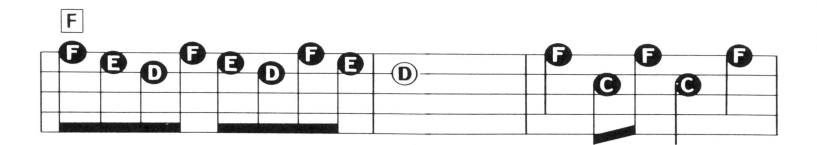

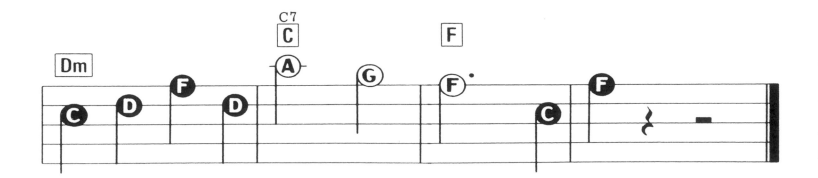